Wormhole
Imbroglio to Disengage
Freedom from Substance Abuse

Author Desiree L Woods
Illustrations by Roshanay Fatima

WORMHOLE
Imbroglio to Disengage
Freedom from Substance Abuse
Copyright 2024©
Library of Congress **Control Number: 2024911941**

All rights reserved. This book or parts thereof,
May not be reproduced in any form without permission with
The exception in the case of brief quotations embodied in critical
article and reviews for promotion.

For information address:
Desiree L Woods
DayMart Textile Services & Outlet, LLC
2785 East Grand Boulevard #150
Detroit, MI 48211
DayMart.services@gmail.com

WORMHOLE | IMBROGLIO TO DISENGAGE
A Grid to Freedom from Crack Cocaine Addiction

Table of Content

DEDICATION
ABOUT THE AUTHOR
PROLOGUE
PREFACE
ROOTS
LET'S TALK
STATISTICS
HER ROOTS
OVERTURE TO DRUG ADDICTION
COMMERCIAL BREAK
OVERTURE
INTERVIEW WITH EX DRUG ADDICT
ANNOTATION
DEE
INTERVIEW WITH EX DRUG ADDICT
DEE
INTERVIEW WITH EX DRUG ADDICT
COMMENTARY
OTHER DRUG STATISTICS AND TRAGEDIES

Table of Content

THEIR STORIES
READING FOR ENCOURAGEMENT
DECLARATIONSPIRITUAL WARFARE
AFFIRMATION
ASSURANCE
GOD IS THE HIGHEST POWER
STRATEGIES TO RECOVERY
COMMENTARY
RESOURCES
CHURCHES

DEDICATION

Let this book be your '**Wormhole**' - a tunnel between two distant points, that cuts the travel time from one point to another: From <u>Addiction to Restoration</u> -from <u>Bondage to Freedom!</u>

If you are sick and tired of riding on a mentally exhausting roller coaster ride; and need to know how to get off that venomous cycle:

Want insight on the gateways and strongholds that have you bound to crack cocaine addiction and the lifestyle;

Want to know how to escape?

This book is dedicated to you. Guaranteed to work, if you work the strategies and apply the principles. Awareness is the key that unlocks the door and it also closes doors…Turn the Key and unlock your liberty!

ABOUT THE AUTHOR

Desiree L. Woods is a Christian writer, Detroit-native with southern roots, entrepreneur, and mentor. She is inspired to write books to help people struggling with issues as further described. She uses her ability to capture the core of the problems and provide comfort, hope and resources. She is the author behind this book Part Three of a Trilogy: 'Wormhole-Imbroglio to Disengage: A Grid to Freedom from Substance Abuse': and 'Part One -Tina–Unexpected Pleasures, Unanticipated Pain – sub tittle 'Abstractions & Hindsight': Addressed to Teen Moms & their Families: Part Two 'GEM: A Positive Commute Ending Domestic Violence'. She is also the author of 'You Can Say That-The Doors We Close', To help you recognize the signs of inappropriate behaviors and to comfort those struggling with sexual trauma in hope of getting past the distresses.

She has experienced sexual trauma, been a Teen Mom; Escaped Domestic Violence and had a bout with Substance abuse, and now is victorious over all those areas, and desires to help others come out triumphantly.

PROLOGUE

WORMHOLE Signifies a shortcut, a tunnel between two distant points being: Crack Cocaine Addiction and Restoration

IMBROGLIO-Crack cocaine can put you in many intricate or complex situations that can be violently confusing or bitterly complicated.

DISENGAGE- to release someone or something to which they are attached or connected to: to remove from an area of conflict.

THE INTENT
The intent is to free you from the lifestyle and addictions. It will take engaging all gateways, the mind, the spirit and the soul along, with one more important factor that I will go into later. There is not a pill you can take, or a detox you can go through. You cannot just embrace therapeutics and not interject spiritual warfare, and you cannot interject the two without the soul of the person having a made-up mind! It takes all above gateways interacting simultaneously to work, and how it can work is laid out herein.

PROLOGUE

Crack Cocaine sat on a wall

Crack Cocaine had a great fall,

and all the avenues, the lustful dreams

and temptations that Crack Cocaine

will tempt you with, and all the dealers,

associates and demonic influences:

couldn't put Crack Cocaine Addiction

back together again!

                That is the purpose of this book!

PREFACE

Crack Cocaine has no respect of person. It does not consider age, race, social or economic status. It has the same destructive stronghold on a CEO, preacher, musician, or prostitute.

It is a gateway. It is very seductive and the strongest diuretic on or off the market. It can give you a feeling of euphoria and also have you completely out of your mind; doing things that you would not normally do if you had control over your will. It is also a hallucinogen and can make your imagination run wild.

It starts off as an inexpensive high and can rob you of your finances, worldly possessions, relationships, house & family.

ROOTS

Listed are roots that may initiate drug usage but could escalate to addiction:

- A person experiencing extreme pain
- Experimenting with drugs
- Sex, loneliness, depression
- Unforgiveness, anger; peer pressure,
- Recreational usage, psychological issues
- Not having a strong spiritual or ethical connection.

Most people that use drugs legal or illegal drugs may have been introduced:

- Through a physician or peer
- For relief of pain,
- To enhance an ability
- For recreational purposes
- A feeling of euphoria
- Temporally forget their problems
- Enhance their senses.

Some roots began by:
- Having drugs in the home
- Easily attainable in the neighborhood, school or work

ROOTS

- Association
- Knowing who can find it
- Knowing who the dealers are
- A close friend, relative or co-worker

These types of relationships could start with usage and end up with addiction.

LET'S TALK

I want you to think about the Roots that intwined you. Know that **roots** are deeply set and can branch out in different phases that can lead to addiction.

There are also **Triggers**- the mechanism that can propel your emotion: you know them: an occasion that you chose to use for escape, such as death of a loved one, something or someone that annoyed you, a trauma such as sexual; a celebration or accident; a scent; a song; or emotion such as hate; jealousy or loneliness!

Stages of dependency and strongholds will be reflected and how to escape; together with approaches that can destroy the stronghold! The focus in this book is Crack Cocaine addiction but the struggles, deliverance and inspirations can apply to almost any addiction. Everybody is different. Some have gone through a 12 Step Narcotics Anonymous Program and received help. Others have obtained support from a relative, therapist or close friend, that's fantastic! For you that are left in the trenches, this is for you.

LET'S TALK

Welcome! These pages will reveal the ugly stronghold of Crack addiction. It takes more than your own self will to get free but to get free an important step to start with is your own self-will, your drive to quit, your provocation for change!
I will also expose some of the ugly 'actualities' a person may experience while using crack cocaine.

If you are a family member of a person using, maybe this information will give insight as how to reach out to them or use it as a tool for discovery and liberation.

There are periods after a person's usage, when they are vulnerable, whereas spent all or used up all their options at that time; and go to a family member or friend and try to express what they have just experienced.

This is the time when a user is most susceptible to change. This is the time where you can use love and intervention not judgement.

STATISTICS

NCDAS Alarming Key Findings
(National Center for Drug Abuse Statistics)

- 50% of 37,309 million people in the United States 12 and older, have used illicit drugs at least once.

- .3% of 37,309 million - Cocaine usage is Youth Ages 12-17

- There have been 700K Drug overdose deaths in the US since 2000 and nearing one million today.

- 21.2% (148,400) are Cocaine Overdoses in United States

FHE Health-Findings
A Nationally Accredited Behavioral Health Program

- Cocaine is the third most used illicit drug in US.
- Annually hospital visits are more than 350,000 times and account for 54% of drug related incarcerations.

MONOLOGUE

Following is a real-life narrative, that chronologize from roots and branch out to triggers, usage and addiction in an ordinary person's life. There is also an interview, some mishaps and statistics, resources featured and more.

Some of you probably have seen it all, the wild parties; illicit sex; irrational mental trips, and manipulations by fake friends. If that is so, it's okay to skip the Narrative and go straight to the remedies and resources.

Yet the stories are helpful to help you to understand transitions and let you know that you are not alone. The emphases on roots and triggers are to help you recognize how they lead to addictive behaviors and how seeing, you can incorporate processes that can bring about complete deliverance.

WORMHOLE | IMBROGLIO TO DISENGAGE
A Grid to Freedom from Crack Cocaine Addiction

HER NARRATIVE

HER ROOTS

She smoked her first cigarette when she was 12 years old. It was a Pall Mall non-filtered cigarette. She was 13 years old when she had her first drink. That was after her Mom would throw a party, and the left over alcohol she would taste.

Her only freedom at a young age was to go to church. She skipped church one Sunday and went near the Brewster Projects to play cards. A Joint was circulated around the room, (she thought it was a rolled cigarette) as she choked almost out of her mind. Everything just got comical. It was on and poppin' after that.

When She was 14, She was introduced to Mescaline, a psychedelic drug, Deb's and other uppers. Her drug usage began recreational and was off and on throughout late teens.

HER NARRATIVE

At one time she thought she was going to be a drug dealer and sold heroin very briefly.

She snorted a pack before bedtime, and it made her calm. She thought it was a good thing until on the 3rd day she got so sick, started throwing up and sweating profusely! That was the end of her using heroine, and her thoughts were; "Something that 'hard' and addictive, she didn't want to ingest or make available to her people". So, that was the end of her using, and she gave up on distribution.

So, all of the above mentioned she could use and still be functional or quit at any time; but the use of Crack Cocaine in her late thirty's was another story! It took three years to figure out the high and five years to get tired of being sick and tired, and found the remedy to liberty!

HER NARRATIVE

From the age of 20-30 she was a sanctified church girl. Her journey began with her searching for God. She was in Manhattan, NY looking up in the sky thinking about God. After she tried a failed attempt to get into the Fashion institute of Technology. Thought she had everything to register but when she arrived in NY, she was told that she didn't have all the information needed and classes had already begun and was told she could start the following year.
That sent her for a loop because that would mean additional time, she would have to spend away from her two children. Moving forward.

A Jamaican friend she met got her into Radio & TV where she monitored the commercials to make sure the advertisers were getting what they paid for. Good job, right? But it didn't last long. The fact that she lied on HR application stating she was the sister of the person that referred her.
Then admitted she wasn't any kin to him, which was grounds for dismissal. Win some, lose some!

HER NARRATIVE

So, she started dancing in the nightclubs which proved quite lucrative. She was always told, "Why are you here? "You don't belong." Not because she couldn't dance, but that her demeaner was more like a 'good girl'. After a couple months of dancing, one day she went shopping bought new costumes, mahogany high heel slippers and another wig.

She was on her way to her hotel (The Taft Hotel) and was approached by a dude. He was attractive, a smooth talker, had her attention. So smooth that when they finished 'Shooting the Breeze', he walked away with her shopping bags and new customs!

She couldn't figure out even today how that happened! That was the end of her dancing career!

After that, she began to travel with a magazine company selling subscriptions of magazine packages that included Ebony, Jet, GQ, etc.

HER NARRATIVE

It was interesting and fun while it lasted. After a while, she got acquainted with a guy that was a leader in the company and he too was talking about leaving but going back to Chicago and wanted her to go with him. He didn't care that she had two children, he just wanted her to be with him. She was young and missing home and kids by then, so she let him down easy, and started her way back home and detoured via Manhattan before Detroit.

One day she was in Manhattan, looking up to the sky and thinking about God. She was approached by a member of Sun Myog Moon's an Occult leader (didn't know it at that time.) Was invited to go to a workshop that lasted for a week, after going to a preliminary weekend meeting. They seemed quite friendly and loving so she agreed.

HER NARRATIVE

Nothing went right at the workshops. There was another workshop that had been in session for some days, and they didn't want her to start in the middle. The host was very apologetic and promised if she come back to the meeting next week, it would be more organized.

Also, to her surprise nothing stayed on her stomach. her bowels were out of control, so the bathroom was her best acquaintance!

She agreed to come back and purchased a book about the leader Sun Myog Moon and bought a round trip bus ticket to Miami, Florida. That would give her time to read up on the organization and something to do until the workshop would start the following week.

Well, that trip gave her enough time to see the light and realized the Moonies (she later found out that is what they were called) were not for her. She thanked God that when you seek Him with a pure heart, you will find Him! She headed back to Detroit!

HER NARRATIVE

She's back in Detroit at her mother's house. This girl kept a portable sewing machine with her wherever she went. Even in New York she was always sewing. A couple of weeks in she had an altercation with a relative. What the fight was about, she doesn't even remember unto this day. She advised him if he hit her, that she would stab him with her scissors. He took his fist and socked her in her eye so hard it turned black and blue (and have a stigma today because of it). So, she stabbed him with her scissors! Both injuries were devastating but no one lost the quality of their life. They hugged and forgave each other as they waited for the ambulance. Her mother was out of town, and she knew how much this person meant to her mother, so she left. She anticipated her mother being upset and would give her time to cool off, she thought.

Well, on return her mother changed the locks on the door and told family not to mention her name ever again in that house!

HER NARRATIVE

She lodged at YWCA on Madison, in Downtown Detroit. The Men's YMCA was on the same street almost side by side to the Women's. After a couple of weeks, she met a young man that asked her why she was there and when she explained it, he told her of his uncle that had a room upstairs for rent and suggested to go look at it. It was on the west side. Later he took her to meet him. His Uncle and wife were Muslims and they took to her right off the bat, and gave her the keys.

This same person also took her to a COGIC church (Church of God in Christ). She had never been in a sanctified Church. That's where she learned how present God is, how powerful He is, and how alive the bible is.

One day it was on a Wednesday. She got a call from John-John saying he was over Royce, and he wanted her to make him a suit, and that she should come take his measurements and get the deposit. So, she caught the bus and went.

HER NARRATIVE

He lived on the west side of Detroit near Wyoming. She went got Royce's measurements, and as she was taking his measurements, he was asking her questions such as "Is John-John your man"? She said, "no". He asked, "Was she intimate with him? She said "No, she's a virgin".

Although she told the truth about her and John John's relationship, she was lying through her teeth because she had two kids at her mother's house: also not knowing that the answers she gave made her the perfect candidate to be a sacrifice for a devil's ritual! She didn't know it then but Royce was a Satan worshiper. Now let's go back. When she first entered the house, she heard a radio upstairs and by the basement door downstairs and both were on two different stations. When she finished taking his measurements, she was seated in the den upstairs. She could hear John-John and Royce arguing. John-John was saying "I told you man, she's yours! She's yours, man!" repeatedly. Also John-John had come upstairs stripped down to his long johns. When he went back downstairs, she picked up the phone and dialed a cab.

HER NARRATIVE

As she was giving the address to the dispatcher the call was lost. She tried to call again, but the phone went dead!
She started saying in her head, "Jesus if you real, be with me right now!!" and began to go down the stairs. She could hear them at the front door now, as she was putting on her coat and shoes, she started saying, "I'm sorry to bother you, soo sorry". At the same time fumbling with the lock on the door with the shotgun to her head, she ran out the door as she was nervously but melodiously singing: "Thank you, Jesus", "Thank you, Jesus", "Thank you, Jesus", "Thank you, Jesus", over and over again until she saw a bus and was thanking God that she didn't get shot in her back!

She didn't know which way the bus was going but she ended up downtown by the City-County Building. She asked the driver if it was alright for her to stay on the bus while he went on break. He agreed. He came back and she headed home.

HER NARRATIVE

The bus let her off at the corner where the church was located. Getting off the bus she could hear the sound of the music. She went and tried the door and it was unlocked. They were having an alter call so she sat on the back pew. She was reminiscing on what she just went through and suddenly ran down the aisle to the front and gave her heart to God!
She felt lightheaded, for once in her life everything looked bright and she was full of joy. Tears was running down her eyes but they were not sad tears but tears of joy! The power of God was so strong on her.

After that meeting with God, she would stay up all night reading the word of God, not only because she was hungry to know more about God but also because she would be bothered by demons when she would fall asleep. It seemed like as soon as she would start nodding off, they would torment her. One time she saw them in a circle saying "Na-na-na-na-na we're going to get you, were going to get you"! And another night she saw the light on her right side, and darkness on her left side and her arms were outstretched and she was being pulled back and forth and back and forth, and it was a figure that

HER NARRATIVE

looked like a large Angel in the light and on the left was thick darkness, and it was a tug of war and the light won then, she woke up! She would stay up all night reading the word until she got strong enough. She learned how to fight the devil with the Word of God. Sometimes she would just say "Get behind me Satan-the Blood of Jesus is against you! or "You can't cross the Blood Line" or "The Blood of Jesus!

One time she felt this presence come in the room and then on her bed, then on her chest and she couldn't say a word! she tried to say Jesus and nothing came out; so, she said it in her mind over and over Jesus - Jesus! And the presence went away! She learned by reading the Word that all powers are ordained by God but He is the highest power! That gave her relief, that gave her power! Furthermore, Jesus said "He gives us power to cast out devils"! She grew being filled with the spirit knowing the Lord in the power and demonstration of the Holy Spirit and rebuking demons!

(This narrative is given so you can see how deep her roots were in Christianity. Crack cocaine don't have no respect of person!

Commercial Break

This is an invitation to contact an agency or organization listed here or in the back of this book under resources.

Listed are national and local resources. Much Success!

Wayne Integrated
Health Network (DWIHN)
Substance Abuse Treatment
Centers
800-241-4949

National Hotline
800-662-help (4357

Shar House
1852 W. Grand Blvd 48208
Admissions
313-894-8444 x2207
800-241-4949 Assessment

Call '211'

Request Shar House

Church resources
International Gospel Center
375 Silliotte Drive
Ecorse, MI 48229
313-389-2700

IGC Services
336 Salliotte
Ecorse, MI 48229
313-383-5500

Christian Center Church
5080 Belmont St.
Hamtramck, MI 48212.
Pastor Elijah Rice.
313-871-3978

Peoples Community Church
8601 Woodward Ace
Detroit, MI 48202
313-871-4676
Pcc8601@ameriteh.net

Redeeming Grace Church
15700 Leroy St
Southgate, MI 48195
734-282-0115
info@redeemingGraceSouthgate.org

One House
614 N. La Brea Ave
Los Angeles, CA 90036
318-763-4521
hello@one.online

New Birth Missionary Baptist Church
6400 Woodrow Rd
Lithonia, GA 30038
770-696-9600
www.newbirth.org

HER NARRATIVE

People were getting set free all around her. Prostitutes were getting saved, drug attacks were being set free without going through withdrawals, and the homeless were coming in and getting saved, healed, fed, clothed, housed and employed! (This was in the late 7O's). The oil ran down from the Pastor to the Parishioners. They laid hands on the sick and they recovered. Yes, that church was working under the anointing of the Holy Spirit. She was even healed of cancer in the 4th stage supernaturally! But the devil got busy and the Jezebel spirit arose strong, you know that seducing, controlling, manipulative spirit. The members started leaving the church. Although God was moving mightily, they were just babes in Christ, and they started looking elsewhere to worship. They all went their separate ways in different groups. She changed churches a couple times and the Spirit was not as high in the services as it was there. Church was more like a social club with its clicks. She got so disenchanted with the behaviors of the 'Aints' and took her eyes off Christ: Said, "If this is Christianity…then I'm walking!".

HER NARRATIVE

This is the conversation she had with God. "Lord I'm not saying I don't want you, just Church folks. She was mad at Christians not Christianity. They're not interested in the poor. They look at the homeless and drug addicts sideways, where is the love! They don't have nothing in place to help the community, and "The straw that broke the camel's back" is, they are arguing about who is going to drive the van that would take me and my children home! They have a brand-new van and nobody wants to drive the van! I can read my bible and praise God at home!" *This was in the early 80's.*

When the unclean spirit is gone out of a man, he walketh through dry places, seeking rest and find none. Then he says, I will return into my house where I came out; and when he comes and find it empty, swept and garnished, then goes he, and takes with him seven other spirits more wicked than himself, and they enter in and dwell there and the last state of that man is worse than the first.   Matthew 12:43-45

WORMHOLE | IMBROGLIO TO DISENGAGE
A Grid to Freedom from Crack Cocaine Addiction

THE INTERVIEW

INTERVIEW WITH AN EX-DRUG ADDICT

Interviewer: What was your life before drugs?

Dee: It was good, I was fulfilling my Dreams. I'm a victor of domestic violence as well. Had several toxic relationships yet, I'm an overcomer. Did a little hair modeling; was designing cloths; doing Braids & Extensions; had a pretty good clientele. Children doing good in school, was in the process of starting several lucrative business deal, no complaints.

Interviewer: Can you touch on being a victor of domestic violence and toxic relationship?

Dee: Well, I predicted the outcome of a few relationships prior to commitment, one ended with me being shot and jumping out a second story window! I predicted the outcome. I met him unknowingly when he was transitioning from a jail sentence where he killed his wife of 20 years: to make a long story short, I made him "mad" as his mother told me not to do, and he shot me point blank execution style in my head and I jumped out

INTERVIEW WITH AN EX-DRUG ADDICT

the second story window of the housing complex. Thank God, I'm alive in my right mind with nothing missing nothing broken. That did not break me!

Dee: Thank God! ...but the relationship that threw me for a loop was the one I had sometime after that: I was reacquainted with a guy that I had a crush on in Junior High School. I predicted how the relationship would end before I got into it. We must learn how to follow that inner voice of peace! and instead of me following my mind, I dismissed it, and low and behold my prediction was right, he was a loser. That is the beginning of when I started beating myself down with unforgiveness. I was sulking in unforgiveness and masking it by using drugs to escape. At first it was marijuana and it worked; it got my creative juices working.

Don't think I didn't meet good candidates for a healthy relationship, that's not true. I settled for the wrong ones. I thought I could fix them, that was stinking thinking! You know what they say...IF it walk like a duck, quack like a

INTERVIEW WITH AN EX-DRUG ADDICT

duck...it's a duck! You can't change nobody, only God can and the best thing for you to do is pray at a distance and keep it moving!

Interviewer: How did you get started using drugs?
Dee: Oh well! I was introduced to crack cocaine by an associate, not a friend, because a friend would not introduce an enemy to Crack Cocaine!

I was looking for marijuana, there was a shortage at that time in the late 80's it was hard to find anywhere. So, at first this person had weed but shortly afterwards due to the shortage, instead of weed, she had crack. I was apprehensive at first, it took her more than a couple times to convince me...that darn weed shortage! She showed me how to smoke it. I thought it was harmless, oh boy was I wrong!

Interviewer: What was the hook?
Dee: I liked the attention; it seemed like some kind of secret sisterhood or brotherhood. Everybody shared and was friendly (at first). The drug dealers treated you like family (at

INTERVIEW WITH AN EX-DRUG ADDICT

first). Being a big spender, you were treated with respect. You don't know in the beginning that the only reason why they are treating you with respect is because you are spending your money.

Also, it is not obvious in the beginning that you have given these people a title like (friend, brother or nephew) that binds you to them, and that lifestyle or relation, and they are not one iotas worthy of it. Not only is the drug a stronghold but the lifestyle is most forbidden, from the drug lords to the dealers to the crack addicted!

ANNOTATION

Let's be transparent. I know how hard it is to tell someone a little white rock is controlling your life and taking you on a downward spiral journey that you can't control! Especially when you were the one that people would come to for advice and help. Particularly if you've been the one 'Voted Most to Succeed' and or was successful. I plead with you to swallow your pride and shame the devil. Get Free!

The incidents written here are true, the names have been changed to protect the innocent. Some content maybe graphic. It's meant to uncover the ugly deceit of crack cocaine and help you understand that the person that is addicted to crack cocaine will do things they wouldn't normally do in their right mind. A strong fixation is enchanting them and overtaking them while they are under the spell. When the drugs wears off, they are back to themselves and either filled with guilt, want to confess, or looking to find another hit.

ANNOTATION

It will make a person a thief, secretly steal from his family, friends or coworkers: or a robber. violently taking what you have, in your face! The stronger the addiction the harder the fall! Your fall can be quick depending on how fast and how large you spend and how suddenly your money dissipates, or how high you have fallen from the societal latter. It can happen slowly or suddenly!

There are circumstances of rape, being battered and held hostage, and some girls have not been found even unto this day.

Crack Cocaine will make you jump out a window, in front of a train and put your children in harm's way, not intentionally but because you are so involved in smoking and getting high: you don't see the deceit that surrounds you and the trouble that is inevitable.

Today there are numerable and attainable Faith Based Programs and Therapeutic assistance. Some are listed in the back of the book.

National Hotline 800-662-help (4357 | Call '211'

WORMHOLE | IMBROGLIO TO DISENGAGE
A Grid to Freedom from Crack Cocaine Addiction

DEE

DEE

The first three years of smoking crack wasn't bad. She could hide it from family and friends. She was still trying to learn what the high was.

Then bam! Suddenly it hit her. She went into another dimension. She felt the absence of the spirit of God; but had the unction to preach! She would start preaching "Jesus is coming soon, you better get ready. Jesus loves you, all you have to do is ask Jesus to come into your heart, to forgive you. There is nothing that you have done that he won't forgive you for. He has a purpose and plan for your life. He will forgive you from all your sins."

On one occasion she heard somebody say, "She knows something, get her! Then she would run out the house and back to her house for safety.

It was a rush, she was preaching and running from demons at the same time. That only made her feel like she had to conquer this! she told herself over and over again, "I can control this."

DEE

She started getting high at home since she had to run home anyway, she thought that would be the best thing to do. One time it was late, and she let two guys in her house, she knew one of them and they went into the basement. Her children were sleeping upstairs on the second floor. Everything was going alright until one pulled out a gun and took advantage of her, took the boom box that was playing and took other valuables in the house. The most hurting part is the Boom Box belonged to her son. When they were done, they headed upstairs, with her at gun point...then they went out the back door grinning. She was outdone! She was glad that her children were safe but she was scared that they might have heard or seen something. She made a decision then to put them out of harm's way!

Another time she was over Charlene's and we were smoking. She laid the glass pipe down and the smoke came up in a shape of a figure walking like a demon! That totally convinced her that she was going to need more than her own self will to get out of this bondage!

DEE

Another time when she was trippin' and they were at the penthouse: she overheard two men say, "Lock her in the bathroom". She ran out the penthouse at the Pavilion down the elevator out the building across Gratiot through Eastern Market to Superior that was about 3½ miles non-stop to her house: it's a wonder that she didn't have a heart attack! Although she had episodes that seemed like God had left her: and spiritual demonic attacks, God always had His angels lead her to safety.

She knows it is true "He will never leave you or forsake you" …Hebrews 13:5

WORMHOLE | IMBROGLIO TO DISENGAGE
A Grid to Freedom from Crack Cocaine Addiction

THE INTERVIEW

INTERVIEW WITH AN EX-DRUG ADDICT

Interviewer: Did you enjoy getting high at all?

Dee: At first it was to pass the time away. Afterward I was trying to get victory and control over the demons it had over me. I would tell myself that "I will not let my imagination run wild, I will not be fearful, and I would not see the spirit of darkness or hear their voices." It failed every time. So no, I did not enjoy getting high, but I was hooked.

Interviewer: What are some of your regrets?

Dee: I don't regret putting my children out of harm's way? The older children well, one was staying with my mother the other was away at school and one was staying with his Godmother. But the younger three children I had no other choice but to let the state take care of them since I had no family support. I picked out the foster parent, made a pact with Brook so it would be easier to see my children and get them on the weekend. She so assured me it was her desire to see my children back home with me as well.

INTERVIEW WITH AN EX-DRUG ADDICT

Interviewer: How did that work?
Dee: Well, it backfired! As soon as she got parental rights she vanished, and my mother kept her where abouts a secret from me as well. Prior to that I had contact with them, I would comb my girl's hair and interact with them and had overnight visits. Then there was no contact at all! That was the hardest thing I ever endured! That lasted for a year but through my sister I found out where they lived.

Of course, my relationship with Brook was strained. But me and my girls agreed that we would have a better relationship when they graduated.

I regret that the experience caused so much damage emotionally and mentally. I think sometimes, maybe I would not have let myself get so entangled in drugs had I kept them at home? Wishful thinking. So, thoughts of, "If I, would've, could've, should've, plagued me. I finally came to the realization to apply Mercy and Grace" to it. If it wasn't for Mercy, it could have been worse, and if it wasn't for His Grace, which was made perfect in my weakness, I would

INTERVIEW WITH AN EX-DRUG ADDICT

not have survived. But the upside is that my girls were well taken care of. Today one is a thriving Hairstylist and the other did 10 years in the Navy, my dreams were lived out in both, the other is doing well by 'society' standards, and I love her deeply. My prayer is that they be healed from every scar that their past experiences, and being separated from me may have caused them.

WORMHOLE | IMBROGLIO TO DISENGAGE
A Grid to Freedom from Crack Cocaine Addiction

THE INTERVIEW

DEE

"Can I be transparent"? She tried finding a Program like NA or AA but every single one she would look up, when she got there, it didn't exist or was over. She tried a therapist, and after she spoke to the therapist, her mouth would drop in amazement, and she would shake her head. The therapist had no resolution for her, except "Goodbye see you next time".

She even went and checked herself into a crises center. Well, she found out she wasn't crazy after spending a weekend in that place, and the best thing for her was to get the hell out of there! She had to call her oldest daughter to get her in and had to call her to get her out!

She tried going to church hoping to get delivered but like she said, the one she was going to was more like a social club and she couldn't get delivered. She did not know how to tell them and if she did, "What would they do?"

She remembered a relative came over to her house one day, he was an ordained minister from that same church.

DEE

She had just hit the pipe so when he came, she was in full blown hysteria.

She let him in, but she couldn't pretend anymore. She asked him to pull the couch out because somebody was behind it. Then she asked him to look behind the curtain. He tried to convince her there was no one there. He saw the fear in her face, and it scared him, and he ran out the door!

Her son had brought a TV and it was in the Livingroom. It had a telephone connected to it but the dial pad was different from a regular TV pad. When her high came down she decided to watch TV stretched out on the floor. The number on the TV was not in the usual order so when she pressed channel 62 (with her eyes closed) to watch the Stories, she got channel 26 the Christian Television Network instead. It's in the late 90's now.

WORMHOLE | IMBROGLIO TO DISENGAGE
A Grid to Freedom from Crack Cocaine Addiction

THE INTERVIEW

INTERVIEW WITH AN EX-DRUG ADDICT

Interviewer: When did the healing start?

Dee: I cried and cried after the incident with the preacher running out the house, and I started talking to God. I was pacing back and forth in my bedroom: I said, "You said all powers are ordained by You, but You are the Highest Power! You said "if I call on You, You will answer", You said "ask and it shall be given", I am asking you to deliver me from Crack Cocaine, You said "Nothing is too hard for You"!

The next thing I know, I had to run to the toilet and started uncontrollably spitting out demons! When I finished, I had counted up to 16 mucus plugs in the toilet, there were so many more, I got scared and flushed the toilet! Good Riddance!

INTERVIEW WITH AN EX-DRUG ADDICT

Interviewer: You did your own exorcism!

Dee: Well, God did it! Yes, Won't He do it!

Interviewer: Then What?

Dee: So later, I was watching Channel 26 the Christian Television Network (CTN) there was a man on the TV and he was inviting me to go to this revival that a Bishop Dwight Pate was running. I saw him on that program, and he began to speak, as if he was talking to me directly; I'm paraphrasing, he said, *"God loves you, and he will take my hurt, pain disappointment, unforgiveness away and give me beauty for my ashes, the oil of joy for mourning, the garment of praise for the spirit of heaviness. He bottles up your tears!*

There is nothing that you have done that God won't forgive you for. He has love and peace that passes all understanding. You can lay your burdens on His shoulders, and he will carry them. He will forgive you of all your sins and throw them in the sea of forgetfulness and remember them no more. Come to Jesus for his yoke is easy and his burden is light".

I received the 'Word' and it was like instantly my emotions were healed. I asked God to forgive me and I forgave myself. I Felt light as a feather, He said come down and get this oil. I'm not going to tell you how to use it, but it's your point of contact with God.

INTERVIEW WITH AN EX-DRUG ADDICT

Interviewer: So, did you go to the revival?

Dee: Yes, I did. I got two bottles of 'the oil'.

I got the oil and said "Lord you said Try you and see! I ran bath water I anointed my head, my ears, my tongue, up my nose, my eyes, poured it in the bath water and said, "Lord as I wash, Lord, you wash me clean." When I got out that tub: I felt different and my mind was renewed, my emotion was healed, and I had no cravings, everything looked brighter. The Lord took the desire for drugs, cigarettes, weed, pills, heroine and Crack Cocaine, He destroyed the yoke! God told me in prayer that it can't be put back together again!

Interviewer: WOW! That's amazing! And you haven't had the taste for drugs since?

Dee: No! I continued to go to the revival it was six weeks. I continued to watch Christian Television. I played tapes of services and listened to Christian music; I went back to church.

Interviewer: So, what was next?

Dee: I was living in the same neighborhood, so drugs were all around me, in my house, the bad influences were still in the neighborhood. The person that was selling drugs was still living in my house: well, I left stayed with a friend for about 4 weeks then, I came back just to officially move out.

INTERVIEW WITH AN EX-DRUG ADDICT

While living there I would walk out of my way to avoid running into old acquaintances. I can tell you God will save you and deliver you in the midst of a bad situation. His Power is that Great!

I listened to the Birk Walker, who was teaching the Sunday School Lesson on Channel 26 and he invited me to come to the Church, Victory Christian Center Church in Hamtramck. I did and have not looked back! I'm Free! I was saved in my living room, delivered in my bedroom, and set free in the bathroom, ain't God Good! Won't He do it!!

WORMHOLE | IMBROGLIO TO DISENGAGE
A Grid to Freedom from Crack Cocaine Addiction

STRATEGIES for RECOVERY

55

STRATEGIES for RECOVERY

When I say forget it, I means that your past won't hold you hostage. Sure, you will be able to tell your story to help somebody come out. But the stories won't stir up desires to use. Those strongholds are destroyed through the Spirit of God and it cannot be put back together! Yes. you may have dreams that will be so real. You probably even handled and smoked dope in your dreams! But God is good. When you wake up, rebuke the devil, call him a liar. Cast those imaginations down and every high thing that exalt itself against the knowledge of God and continue walking in the strength and Victory with God!

COMMENTARY

Some things cannot not be shared in this type of setting. The reason why these Narratives are written, is so that you would recognize the depth of the strongholds and the dangers that come with it, as well as the pipeline of people that are affected by it. So that you could understand that a person is absolutely unable to help themselves while under the influence and if you have a loved one that is addicted to crack or any other drug: I hope you have found insight and an alternative for healing when all else has failed.

I had no one I could turn to for help but there was a platform The Christian Television Network Channel 26 owned by Glenn Plummer, and the show, The Lesson presented by Glenn Plummer and the two that assisted him at that time, his dear friends Birk Walker and Bishop Dwight Pate.

There were churches I transitioned through that was helpful for that time. Straight Gate Church, Bishop Merrit, High Praise Cathedral (now called)-Bishop Haddon-where Bishop Dwight Pate ran the revival. I am sharing my testimony because if you absolutely have no one to turn too: you can turn to Jesus Christ, speak the Word of God and it will deliver you!

COMMENTARY

I was invited to go to Victory Christian Center Church, a small church in Hamtramck where Pastor Jessie Rice is the Founding Pastor. I received a lot of love at that church from pastor, and his sisters who took me in as family. That was very important for me at that time because I was disconnected from all family members and friends. You don't have to be born in a family for them to become family!

TBN a Christian Broadcasting network had on their format, Bishop TD Jakes, Bishop Miles Monroe and others that I listened to, that was very instrumental in me staying saved: and of course, Christian music. It doesn't matter the genre if it is uplifting and inspirational: this key was significant in me keeping my sanity and helping me to stay focused during those days and nights of transition. When family is not available Jesus was there. The right Music really does tame the savage beast!

COMMENTARY

Most of all because of the Father, Son and Holy Ghost and his ministering Angels, the Word of God (Holy Bible), the obedience of the Ministers of God, the vehicle of Christian TV and me being sick and tired of being 'sick and tired', along with my will to submit to God, I am Free!

Today there are a lot of places and people in place where you can get help in crisis. Some of them are listed in the back of this book.

Commit to know the Word of God and you will come to know God. The Word of God is your defense because it is strong, true and never fails: How then shall they call on him in whom they have not believed? and how shall they believe in him of whom they have not heard? and how shall they hear without a preacher? Romans 10:14.

Stay in the center of people on a productive pathway, just remember nobody's perfect. Get busy and be the best you can be. Connect to a Faith Based organization. Make a total U-turn. I won't say everything will be easy, but you will be better equipped to handle whatever comes your way.

COMMENTARY

Of course, the enemy will come with his tricks, but laugh in the face of the devil and his tactics and stay focused.

It is important to get to know the Word of God and you will get to know Him. His ways are not like our ways, but He is powerful all seeing, all knowing and everywhere. Apply his Word to your life and be joyous and free. It's as simple as that when you incorporate all three gateways (mind soul and spirit) Listed in this book are Narratives to deliverance but staying free is a lifestyle.

I pray that you find resources, people and places in your area that can help and assist you in your recovery. Google

'Substance Abuse Recovery Programs,

'Substance Abuse Counseling'

'Substance Abuse and Therapist'

'Faith Based Substance Abuse Recovery'

'Faith Based Substance Abuse Therapist'

'Non-Profit Agencies for Substance Abuse and Therapy'.

'Faith Based Agencies for Substance Abuse and Treatment'.

You will find your way!

WORMHOLE | IMBROGLIO TO DISENGAGE
A Grid to Freedom from Crack Cocaine Addiction

STATISTICS | TRAGEDIES

OTHER DRUG STATISTICS AND TRAGEDIES

Fentanyl is a synthetic opioid similar to morphine but 100 times more potent.

Illicit fentanyl is smuggled in the United States and mixed with other drugs to increase potency, can be consumed in every way possible and <u>as little as 2 grams can be fatal!</u>

(Exserted from DEA's website)

www.dea.gov/resources/facts-about-fentanyl

THEIRS STORIES

A relative was found dead by associates that were in the house with her, female 27 years old with one child under 5. Drugs were the root cause but the details were not revealed due to her grandmothers wishes.

This same Female's son at age 26, twenty two years later and in another state; was talking to his cousin on the phone (both in different states, stating he was going to try Fentanyl and got it from a reliable source, so it was safe, so he thought. His cousin begged him not to take it. He took it while using the bathroom on the phone, one pill. He threw the phone down and began to run out the house with his pants down (that is how instantly the drug worked): he died on the front lawn. Some people believe he was trying to make it to his car to go to the hospital. Never made it!
This was a regular person, got his education, a house and a car, a job, his reputation was decent, and he was not known as a drug user or distributor. Just one stupid experiment cost him his life!

THEIRS STORIES

Another person I knew tried Fentanyl and it took four attempts with Narcan to bring him back. Thank God he was at the clinic when he took the drug; unknowingly to the staff, but they recognized what was happening and proceeded. No one person would have had enough overdose kits to rescue him had it happened anywhere else. Just one pill caused so much devastation!

Another person, his drug of choice is weed, alcohol and cocaine, have had five Heart related Stent Surgeries because of his drug use.

Another person was using prescription drugs, alcohol, weed and cocaine and have had seizures that has affected his ability to work.

There is no good thing that can come out of Drug Abuse. Seek help to Quit, before it is too late!

THEIRS STORIES

This person grieved for 20 years on the birthday of her brother that was violently killed. Would celebrate with drinking and friends. The last celebration after leaving friends and family she continued alone drinking and grieving. She was found days later dead.

We are talking about recognizing your triggers and not letting them take you to that place of addiction.

WORMHOLE | IMBROGLIO TO DISENGAGE
A Grid to Freedom from Crack Cocaine Addiction

ANTHOLOGIES

THE WHITE HORSE

Do you want to ride the white horse

Do you wanna glide through the high

Do you want to experience my unforgettable high

Do you want to die at the hit of my device

Do you want your breath to exchange for this abuse

Do you want to further my mission too,

By bringing your family and friends to me.

Do you want to kill, or be killed at the expense of

wanting and needing to purchase me!

by Maria Denise

THE BATTLE

Do you know why it is such a battle?

Do you know why bad things happen to good people?

Let me tell you why. First of all, it started before we were created, before God blew the breath of life and man became a living soul.

Yes, God created good and evil, when he created Lucifer,

who thought he would put his seat

above the throne of God!

How crazy is that; but a third part of heaven

was also deceived. Guess what?

They got kicked out! Him and his imps!

Oh my God, Satan fell from Heaven as lightning,

and his kingdom has an expiration date!

So, God took a break and created man, and he was good.

Man was created with a free-will.

He was protected from evil if he would simply obey.

THE BATTLE

In Eden man (Adam) became disobedient.

Yea, Satan tempted Eve to eat from

the 'Tree of Knowledge of Good and Evil.

Girlfriend took the fruit and gave Adam, and he did eat.

Their eyes were opened, and he was ashamed.

God said wait a minute, y'all got to go!

Just in case they would eat from the tree of life

in that precarious state.   Genesis 3:1-23

You see, man was created to worship God,

and God is a gentleman who desires volitional praise.

So, man he gave the power of choice.

Chose you this day whom you will serve.

The Almighty God – Everlasting Life; or

Satan – Son of perdition and eternal damnation.

THE BATTLE

So why do bad things happen to good people?

It all stems from a choice not necessarily yours!

Somebody chose evil, and it came to your door,

it knocked on your door, and you opened it.

It came down your avenue, and you stepped into it.

It walked down your boulevard, and side swiped you.

Unknowingly you got tricked.

Unsuspectingly it came to your door,

and set up shop: with addiction, depression, loneliness,

thoughts of suicide and unforgiveness, murder and

entrapment, confusion, despair, and sickness.

Listen to this, God knew Satan would

cause havoc with His beloved, that's us.

So, he took part of himself and mixed it with flesh.

THE BATTLE

So that he could completely understand

the plight of man and not wipe us out

entirely, along with Satan.

This is Jesus, the Word that was with God in the beginning!

Who is our negotiator, who gives us his Holy Spirit,

our indwelling power, our Comforter and guide.

Check this out, when we except the Word of God

we have the connection to God,

we have overcoming power and restoration.

He is our Battle Axe against the wiles of the enemy,

the very present help in a time of trouble;

and trouble will come-but we win in the end!

THE BATTLE

If you don't know this… the devil knows it:

That God so loved you, that he wrapped himself

in flesh and blood to give you power.

That if you open your eyes and believe,

life and love without end is yours.

So why do bad things happen to good people?

It's because we are on the enemy's hit list.

If you don't know this, the devil knows,

in God we are protected and we win in the end!

So chose you this day, whom you shall serve –

Life or death?

Death and hell were not made for you or me.

Through the deception of the 'Wicked One',

hell has enlarged itself…Chose Life!

THE BATTLE

Immorality may influence you or be around you

but trust in your Protector.

You may eventually experience the first death.

Your body will decay because of Satan's tricks

but your spirit will live because of your choice.

Whether your transition is death, Judgment,

or the Rapture know this: that Jesus is coming again,

and he won't be meek this time!

The Angels are going to make so much noise,

and God is going to sound the trump so loud,

that folks will wake from their grave!

It will be so strong, that we who are alive

our spirit will be drawn to him like a magnet!

We will meet Him in the atmosphere at the halfway point;

THE BATTLE

and we will see him as He is

in all of His Glory and forever be with Him.

Know this…All things work together for good

Let this hope be in you! Jesus is coming Soon!

You better be ready!

                                          1 Thessalonians 4:16

RESOURCES

I invite you to contact an agency or organization listed in this book under resources. Listed here are national and local resources.

NATIONAL HOTLINE

800-662-HELP (4357)

Detroit Wayne Integrated Health Network (DWIHN)Substance Abuse Treatment Centers
800-241-4949

IGC Services
336 Salliotte,
Ecorse, MI 48229
313-383-5500

Shar House
1852 W. Grand Blvd 48208
Admissions
313-894-8444 x2207
Assessment 800-241-4949

Through contacting to the resources listed here is a start. They will assess and determine whether outpatient, inpatient treatment or detox is the appropriate treatment, or if therapeutic counseling will suffice; or even assignment of a mentor. I recommend that you start somewhere. If your situation requires a safe place, please let the intake person know.

COMMENTARY

I had no choice but to trust God. Previously it was explained how through Steps of Faith in God, receiving His word through a preacher my emotions were healed. Affirming God's Word gave me power: the Point of Contact to God through using the Anointed Oil immediately gave me power and deliverance. It broke the yoke, How? I don't know exactly but the yoke was destroyed. The desire was gone! I held on to a bag of weed for two weeks because I thought I would need something to lift my spirit. After two weeks I flushed it down the toilet. I didn't need it anymore! God's Spirit filled me! I had peace, I could think straight, I could see things clearly for what they were. I could define good from evil. I wanted to do the things that would keep me delivered: declaring God's Word, daily affirmations and prayer, gave me power and kept me in relationship. I changed my route when going out, and dropped people like touching a hot skillet that were in that lifestyle. I took on a courage that I never had. I would go to get gas as the gas station and ask for a pack of Winston's non menthol and would apologize to the clerk after he got them saying, "I'm sorry, put those back I quit, force of habit! I could be talking on the phone and start looking for a cigarette and stop in my tracks and say 'Oh no, I'm delivered! By Faith the yoke of bondage was broken through the power of the Holy Spirit, my Comforter, that dwelt in me, working through me and all around me. He reminded me that I was delivered and I gained emotional release every day. You are going to have to fight! It's a spiritual fight, sometimes I woke up having dreams that was so real like I was smoking dope and getting high! I would wake up happy it was a dream and rebuke that spirit to get behind me! There are no chains holding me and Praise God! No Desire! I'm Free. I didn't dwell on that dream and moved on. That meant what happened to me, what the devil meant for evil cannot touch or control me anymore; the entrapment the enemy planned for me is cancelled! Spiritually I know who I am in God, I am connected! Mentally in Jesus name I can handle anything that comes my way; every problem has a solution and I am a winner!

That Comforter is also a Battle Axe through the Blood of Jesus Christ and will destroy your enemies or make them be at Peace with you!

We have a host of Angels that encamp around us waiting for the okay from the Father to move on our behalf and release our Blessings.

The roadmap to staying delivered is to continue to walk in faith and connect to Godly People and Faith Based organizations, and to 'Pass it Forward' once you have been strengthened! And that's what I am doing Clean since 1998 and have not been back! It will work if you work it!

WORMHOLE | IMBROGLIO TO DISENGAGE
A Grid to Freedom from Crack Cocaine Addiction

AFFIRMATIONS | DECLARATIONS

READING FOR ENCOURAGEMENT

If you want to know Him, I suggest you read the whole chapter of St John 14 & 15. John Chapter 14 leads with, let not your heart be troubled: you believe in God, believe also in me... John 14:1

John Chapter 15 leads with, If you abide in me, and my words abide in you, you shall ask what you will, and it shall be done unto you.   John 15:7

Read the Psalms if you want to know how to pray or an idea of how to talk to God and the power of Praise. Read the Gospels to know of Christ. Read the Epistle to know how we should conduct ourselves: when you finally get a chance read the bible from Old Testament you will see how powerful and merciful and longsuffering God is as well as how terrible he can be against evil. Well why does evil seem to be prevalent now? God gave the devil a chance to rule and a time frame, he loses this fight, Amen!

The New Testament to know the embodied Christ who he is and come to know, He is the Door we need to walk through;

and although God has the power to destroy the evil right now, He's a gentle also and gives us the power of choice, 'Chose you this day, whom you will serve." You will find reading Revelations, that it will tell you of past, present and future at any given point. Happy Reading!

DECLARATION

I am who God say I am,

I can do what God say I can do.

I am more than a Conqueror.

I am strong, I am beautiful, I am wonderfully and fearfully made.

I will not fear what man can do to me.

I am the head and not the tail,

Above only and not beneath.

I can do all things through Christ

which strengthens me.

No weapon that is formed against me shall prosper; every tongue that shall rise against me in judgement, shall be condemned!

I'm blessed in the city, my body is blessed,

My mind is blessed, my plans are blessed,

My steps are ordered by God,

The devil is defeated, God is exalted,

I am strong in the Lord and in the power of

His might. My Business is prosperous,

I'm a lender not a borrower in Jesus Name.

WORDS for SPIRITUAL WARFARE

I bind the devil's power out of my atmosphere and cast him out of my house in the name of Jesus, and I speak prosperity and thoughts of good and not evil: I am walking in the spirit and not in the flesh. My steps are ordered by God
I am walking in the resurrection Power of God.
His goodness and mercy shall follow me all my days.
I bind the spirit of fear and confusion, and I speak Peace and a sound mind.
I bind the spirit of addiction off me, my family and cast it out of my atmosphere.
I bind the spirit of lackadaisical and I speak enthusiasm, creativity, and the energy to fulfill the tasks that are set before me.
My body shall function as it was created. All systems shall operate in harmony as they were created to do. My mind is regulated and will function as it should. My sleep is sweat, and I shall awaken afterward refreshed. I am bold and alert. I can do all things through Christ which strengthens me.

AFFIRMATION

I have a great team, we are powerful in our endeavors for business, I am strong spiritually, naturally and emotionally, I am successful. My family is blessed, my children are blessed on down to ten generations. We walk in forgiveness and strength. The spirit of suicide will have to flee out of our atmosphere; depression has no room here. Our family is strengthened with love for one another.

No accidents or incidents around me or my family or my church family. No weapon formed shall prosper!

I walk in newness of life in Jesus Name Amen.

ASSURANCE

Romans 8:37-39

In all these things I am more than conquerors through him that loved me. For I am persuaded, that neither death, nor life, nor angels, nor principalities, nor powers, nor things present, nor things to come. Nor height nor depth, nor any other creature, shall be able to separate me from the love of God, which is in Christ Jesus my Lord.

GOD IS THE HIGHEST POWER

Romans 13:1

Let every soul be subject unto the higher powers, for there is no power but of God: the powers that be are ordained of God.

OUR FIGHT

Ephesians 6:12

For we wrestle not against flesh and blood, but against principalities, against powers, against the rulers of the darkness of this world, against spiritual wickedness in high places.

OUR WAR CLOTHS

Put on the whole armor of God, that you may be able to stand against the tricks of the devil...

For this reason, we put on the whole armor of God that you may be able to endure in the evil day and having done all to stand: Stand therefore having your sexual desires controlled in fidelity.

Your heart structured in honorable principles.

Your feet covered with the revelation of Jesus Christ and peace.

Above all taking the shield of faith wherewith you shall be able to quench all the fiery projectiles of the wicked.

And take the helmet of redemption – knowing we are bought with the precious blood of Jesus therefore we are heirs in God.

And the Sword of the Spirit which is the Word of God!

Praying with all prayer and supplication in the Spirit and watch...

Remember:

Ephesians 6:11-18 - Colossians 1:16,17, - Romans 13:1

This battle is not ours, but the Lords, and we win!

Wormhole
Imbroglio to Disengage
Independence from Crack Cocaine

I will not be apologetic for sharing the word of God and behaviors required through God for deliverance. I speak that I know and testify of what I have seen. I know unequivocally that this route can free a person from any addiction. But the underlining subject herein is about Crack Cocaine or Cocaine. The hardest drug to get free from.

***I beg with all my heart that you never try Fentanyl, a tiny dose is a high dose that can kill you. I know of only 1person that took 1 pill and only survived because he did it at the clinic and the clinicians saw him slumped over and began treatment because he was unresponsive and it took 4 kits of Narcan to bring him back to consciousness. It's a miracle that he is still alive.

988 Suicide & Crisis Lifeline 24/7

Below are listed Steps for Recovery. I promise you, if you apply all the steps, strategies and antidotes listed throughout this book, you will be freed of crack cocaine addiction permanently!

WORMHOLE | IMBROGLIO TO DISENGAGE
A Grid to Freedom from Crack Cocaine Addiction

STRATEGIES FOR RECOVERY

STRATEGIES for RECOVERY

If you have or not have tried other means, I implore you to try the divine route to breaking the chains of crack cocaine addiction.

Step one

Recognize the <u>roots</u> such as: experimenting with drugs; pain; peer pressure? **Roots**- the basic cause; the beginning ventures or attachments that led to something stronger or greater. What are your roots?

_____
_____
_____
_____
_____
_____
_____
_____
_____
_____
_____
_____

Step Two
Triggers is the mechanism that propelled you in the direction toward using. It could also be a person, place, or thing or an emotion such as grief, depression, loneliness. Is it anger, unforgiveness, trauma, or celebrating? What are your triggers?

_____
_____
_____
_____
_____

When you can't find people in your inner circle that you can trust:

3) Accept Jesus Christ as the Son of God and the Savior of your soul.

You can simply do this by saying: *Jesus come into my heart forgive me for all my sins, I accept you as my Redeemer and Lord. Save me from all unrighteousness. And lead me in a right path. I submit my ways to you...*

You are now in the family of God!

STRATEGIES to RECOVERY

4) Forgive those that have offended you and forgive yourself. *Forgiveness is for you, so that you can move on! 1 John 1:9 if we confess our sins, he is faithful and just to forgive our sins: and cleanse us from all unrighteousness:*

I forgive _____ for _____

_____

_____ and

I forgive myself for _____

_____

_____

5) Find a man or woman dedicated to God and a Church that has outreach amenities. Someplace where the power of deliverance is: or a person such as a therapist, preacher or mentor to help hold you accountable, as you walk this walk. God is powerful enough to deliver you in any situation.

Name: _____ number _____

Name: _____ number _____

STRATEGIES to RECOVERY

<u>I was forgiven and healed in my living room, delivered in by bedroom, and set free in my bathroom</u>... but I still had to surround myself with positive, sincere, and loving people of God. Change my association. You will know if you are in the right place because you will feel conviction but not condemnation. Keep your eyes on Jesus! There is no perfect church, but you can find what is perfect for you. When you cannot change your environment immediately, God can change you in your environment, and fill you with his spirit, so that what is around you, can't affect you. Eventually you will need someplace where the people will entreat you with love, as well as strong in the Word of God (Bible). But if there is no one you can turn too, turn to Jesus!

The enemy may come and try to bring the same thing that ran you from the church, in your face. Rebuke it, put it under your feet. Call him a liar and keep it moving!

This is where your declaration come into existence.

STRATEGIES to RECOVERY

6) You can speak the Word of God out loud with authority and Declare the Word of God! Such as I did: for example: <u>You said,</u> *"All powers are ordained by You, but You are the Highest Power!* <u>You said</u> *"if I call on You, You will answer",* <u>You said</u> *"ask and it shall be given", I am asking you to deliver me from Crack Cocaine,* <u>You said</u> *"Nothing is too hard for You!"* Find it in the Word of God and declare it.

I dare you! **Proverbs 8:17** <u>I love them that love me: and those that seek me early shall find me.</u>

Romans 13:1, <u>Let every soul be subject unto the higher powers. For there is no power but of God. The powers that be are ordained of God.</u>

Acts 2:21, <u>AND IT SHALL COME TO PASS, THAT WHOSOEVER SHALL CALL ON THE NAME OF THE LORD SHALL BE SAVED</u> **Matthew 7:8,** <u>For everyone that asks receive: and he that seeks find, and to him that knocks it shall be opened.</u> **Luke 1:37,** <u>For with God nothing shall be impossible.</u> David said: **Psalm 86:7** <u>In the day of trouble I will call upon you: for you</u>

STRATEGIES to RECOVERY

will answer. **Psalms 91:15** <u>I will be with you in trouble; I will deliver you, and honor you.</u> **Isaiah 65:24** <u>and it shall come to pass, that before they call, I will answer; and while you are yet speaking, I will hear.</u>

I called on God to stand by His Word and spoke the Word of God and applied it to my circumstances and God honored His Word and delivered me.

7) Surround yourself with positive people.

I avoided the people that I was associating with when using drugs, if it meant taking a different route to the store, work or church.

Although the relative that was in my house had drugs, God gave me enough strength not to succumb to the temptation. I also made a conscious decision to change my environment. I left and stayed with a friend briefly, then I moved out the neighborhood.

8) You must read or regurgitate the word of God and apply it to your situation.

9) Once you are delivered you must continue to be proactive in your deliverance, until it becomes easy until it becomes natural.

I saw your face in the future and you look much better than you look right now!

Commentary

I started working with faith based and non-profit organizations. I initially worked in administration at the Teen Moms Program at DRMM. Then I advance to Life Skills Counselor, Case Management and Job Development for the men at Oasis. Also worked with Women and children in Transitional Housing at Genesis House II and later worked with Transition of Prisoners (TOP) as Executive Secretary.

You can work in any area that is rewarding even if it is Janitorial, Landscaping or Banqueting services: Customer Service, Uber, Housekeeping, etc. Just do it with your head up and a determined mind. If you are a business owner, have you thought about giving back into the community, whether it is mentoring or investing in programs.

After awhile, you will forget what you've been through. It will be as if it never happened. After we come out, we can pull somebody else out! God will make you look like it never happened! Whatever the unreversible consequences are God's Grace is sufficient, they won't hinder the blessings of God or the joy that is set before us.

RESOURCES

In whatever country, city or state that you are in, you can web search:

Faith Based Substance Abuse Center

Deliverance Church

Faith Based Substance Abuse Counseling

Healing Ministries

Gospel Centered Self Help Organizations

Community Outreach Ministries

Substance Abuse Outpatient Treatment

Substance Abuse Inpatient Treatment

RESOURCES

24 Hour National Hotline
Substance Abuse|
Suicide Prevention|
Veterans|
LGBT up to 25
Dial: 988

Teem Wellness
Substance Abuse & Mental Health
Wayne County, Southgate, Westland
313-396-5300

Detroit Wayne Integrated
Health Network
Substance Abuse   Treatment Centers
800-241-4949

Shar House
1852 W. Grand Blvd 48208
Admissions
313-894-8444 x2207
800-241-4949 Assessment
Request Shar House
through SAMHSA

Substance Abuse and Mental Health Services
Administration
800-662-HELP (4357)

Call '211'

Mentoring Center – <u>Anonymous</u>
12:00pm Saturdays
392 Salliotte
Ecorse, MI 48229

CHURCHES

International Gospel Center
375 Silliotte Drive
Ecorse, MI 48229
313-389-2700

IGC Services
336 Salliotte Drive
Ecorse, MI 48229
313-383-5500

Victory Christian Center Church
5080 Belmont St.
Hamtramck, MI 48212.
Pastor Elijah Rice.
313-871-3978

Peoples Community Church
8601 Woodward Ace
Detroit, MI 48202
313-871-4676
Pcc8601@ameriteh.net

Redeeming Grace Church
15700 Leroy St
Southgate, MI 48195
734-282-0115
info@redeemingGraceSouthgate.org

One House
614 N. La Brea Ave
Los Angeles, CA 90036
318-763-4521
hello@one.online

New Birth Missionary Baptist Church
6400 Woodrow Rd
Lithonia, GA 30038
770-696-9600
www.newbirth.org

www.ingramcontent.com/pod-product-compliance
Lightning Source LLC
Chambersburg PA
CBHW011550070526
44585CB00023B/2534